Weekends

Weekends

Great Ideas
for Memorable
Adventures

Hanoch McCarty
Sidney B. Simon

Health Communications, Inc.
Deerfield Beach, Florida

Library of Congress Cataloging-in-Publication Data

McCarty, Hanoch, 1940-
    Weekends: great ideas for memorable adventures /
Hanoch McCarty, Sidney B. Simon.
        p.   cm.
    ISBN 1-55874-300-6: $10.00
    1. Family recreation. I. Simon, Sidney B. II. Title.
GV182.8.M33   1994   94 -1520
790.1'91—dc20   CIP

Publisher: Health Communications, Inc.
                3201 S.W. 15th Street
                Deerfield Beach, Florida 33442-9879

Cover design by Barbara Bergman

Acknowledgments

There are many people we must thank for their roles in the preparation of this book: Patricia Hammond for her kind support so long ago when the idea for this book germinated; Rosemary and Harry Wong for their sterling example of joyous balance between work and play; Michael Wenger for his special role in our lives as a great friend to play with.

Of course, I must thank my dear wife Meladee who is my play-partner and co-conspirator.

Above all, I must acknowledge and thank my co-author, mentor and life-long friend, Sidney Simon. His role in my life cannot be overstated. He began as my teacher, became and remains my mentor, and grew into my deepest and most consistent friend. His courageous questioning and creative suggestions became the seed which grew into this book. He has planted many seeds for me: I have found the alternatives to a blah life through the questions he asks and the model he is. Thank you forever, Sid.

Hanoch McCarty

Of course, I must thank my dear wife Suzanne who is my co-partner and play-conspirator.

As all good students do, Hanoch has taught me much. As all good friends do, he has added light and joy to my life. He is a man who can find cracks in the gray wall of blandness that sometimes surrounds everyone's life, and has often helped me break through this wall to the garden beyond filled with sunshine and the bounty of flowers. A great deal of our friendship is contained within these pages, so rather that say more I will read our book again and savor what we have created together.

Sidney B. Simon

To my dear brother,
Douglas Bendell, whose kindness and
inventiveness helped to create many memorable
weekends, vacations, great escapes and family gatherings.
By creating events around which family memories will
always center, he is a great model and mentor for everyone.
From Cairo to Kansas, from Esalen to the
Top of The World, Doug has always led the way.

And to my dearest mother,
Jean McCarty, who taught us the value
of work and the necessity of balancing it with
the sustenance of play. She had an endless
imagination for the most interesting things to do,
the most horizon-expanding places to go, and
the most unusual, thought-provoking
ways to get there!

— Hanoch McCarty

To Suzanne, my wife:
The most playful human being
I know, who makes every weekend
a celebration.

— Sidney B. Simon

Contents

THINKING AHEAD:
What Do You Want To Do
. . . To Get . . . To Be?

We learned from our friend Merrill Harmin an idea he calls "Do-Get-Be." This is a way of becoming really clear about our use of leisure time.

When we look forward to a weekend, holiday or vacation, we usually think of what we are going to *do*. Almost all of the planning is focused on the doing — what we'll do, what the alternatives are, when we'll do it, how much it will cost, where to get the tickets.

So we experience many events as a series of tasks, problems, chores, steps. Thanksgiving is coming. We send invitations, clean the house, buy the turkey and trimmings, begin cooking and preparing all the food, set the table. While this is going on, sometimes we forget to be joyful. The tasks get to us. We might find ourselves being impatient or even angry with a spouse or a child: "Get out of my kitchen while I'm cooking!" The focus is *always* on what we're *doing* and are going to *do*.

Merrill suggests we ask a new question: "What do you want to **get** from Thanksgiving?" What a deceptively simple question! For it gets right to the heart of what this event is all about. What, indeed, do we really want from it? Ah, I want to get closer to my family, we might say. I want to create a joyous time that will build warm memories for all of us. I want my children to reconnect with our far-flung relatives and see the good people with whom they are connected. I want a time of peace. I want to be truly and humbly thankful for all the good in my life.

As we look at our frantic preparations, we need to ask ourselves, "Will rushing, bustling, getting nervous or being impatient get us all those things?" And the answer is plain. We don't feel warm and close when behaving like this.

So Merrill asks the key question, "How do I have to **be** in order to get what I want?" What sort of being am I demonstrating? Which aspects of my personality should come to the fore? To get closer to to my loved ones on that Thanksgiving day, I have to be calmer, warmer, friendlier — more focused on the people I'm with and less on how well the dinner table looks. I have to go slower, be more gentle, do more listening.

How many evenings, planned with delightful anticipation, turn sour because we lose sight of "being" in the rush of preparation? How many vacations, looked forward to with months of desire, turn flat because of nerve-wracking speed on the highway with the radar detector bleeping or the anger generated by the difficulty of parking the station wagon? In our rush to do, do, do, we forget what we really want to get and, most importantly, how we have to be in order to get it.

As you work more and more with the Do-Get-Be concept, it will become clearer to you what it is that you want to get from this and any other experience.

We think it's important for you to be clear in the beginning about what it is you want to get, so you can be the person who gets it.

Merrill Harmin makes the point that we are fully in charge of how we are in any experience. We can be gloomy, we can be sour, we can be cynical. All of those are possible. But we can also be open. We can be adventuresome. We can be connective to the other people in our lives. We can be playful, we can be sensitive, we can be good listeners, we can be risk sharers. As you begin to think of the Saturday nights and Sunday afternoons ahead, how do you want to *be*?

So we urge you to ask yourself: what is there to *do*,

what do I want to *get* out of it and how must I *be* to get it?

Then go for it.

PART I

Extraordinarily Relaxing

Friday Nights

T.G.I.F.

Friday nights have a lot to do with how the weekend turns out. Thank God It's Friday!

Some Friday nights are a prelude to a scheduled event and can be used for planning or packing. Others are merely another leisure night to play with — the visit to a bar with colleagues before the trek home; a quick meal-and-a-movie; the ubiquitous boob tube and a beer. And certainly Friday nights can carry high energy: Dance time!

Friday nights, though, may also have a restorative quality. When the week has been especially tough and demanding — for yourself or someone you love — you can use it as a gentle retreat from worldly concerns, and a chance to restore body and spirit so the rest of the weekend becomes usable, not the typical blur of dragging your tired bones around in pointless circles.

The simplest Friday night activity is also the most obvious: Go home and go to sleep. Certainly you can plunk your buns down in front of the TV and call it restful. We think, however, that a little planning will make for an especially relaxing Friday night, one that will bring real rejuvenation.

Unless you are one who absolutely has to be in contact with others to feel good, limiting contact can help. This is a time to disconnect phones and turn on answering machines.

If you have children, you might negotiate a "baby-sitting trade agreement" with friends or neighbors. You take their kids for a weekend night to be returned the next morning after 9 A.M., and they reciprocate some other weekend. We've even done this for a whole week (ah, what saints we were), taking their son while our friends went to Jamaica for their holiday. Our week came recently when Hawaii beckoned. This arrangement lowers both cost and guilt!

Following are some other things to make your Friday nights restorative (and memorable).

Curl Up With A Good Book

A way to make this special is to buy books in advance. Beside your bed, maintain a short stack of unread but eagerly anticipated novels for moments such as these.

Purchase books by your favorite authors and save them for these nights.

Re-read an old favorite to savor and renew your memories of its special flavors.

Get Or Give A Massage

Arrange for a qualified (licensed) massage therapist to come to your home for a full massage. We recommend the general massage rather than the therapeutic massage because the general is more gentle — it has fewer moments of discomfort. But go for the therapeutic if your kinks and knots are screaming at you.

People who really know how to take care of themselves are no strangers to massage. Many own their own massage tables!

You can find a really good massage therapist through a local health club.

You can give a gift certificate to a friend who really needs some rest and repair. A massage is a message of true caring.

Partners who care for each other can read a good how-to book on message and learn to massage each other. Favorites for us include a scalp massage (often done as an extended shampoo) and a foot massage. It pays to use a massage oil — scented or not. Coconut oil works just wonderfully.

This is a nonsexual massage unless the partners agree otherwise. It's not relaxing to think you've got to "pay" for this sensual experience with a sexual one. If you want to do a sexual massage, that's different and lots of fun — if you've agreed beforehand.

Take A Bath

Go to the tub, pour in a "detox" formula of two pounds of Epsom salts and one pound of baking soda. Make the water as hot as you can stand and soak away your troubles. Bring a book if you like. Add some music from your portable cassette player (battery powered only, of course, and placed away from the water).

Some city dwellers are fortunate to have a service that rents portable hot tubs on trailers. These are delivered right to your backyard set up and ready to go, on a trailer which is anchored and stable. They are wonderful for parties — Saturday night — but it's not that much more to rent it for two nights and have it all to yourself (or alone with your partner) for a preview on Friday night.

Another bath refinement can be found in a local hotel. Many have "health spas" with sauna, whirlpool, steam room, etc. Hotels that are not in resort areas depend on weekday business travelers and are often underfilled on weekends. Most of them attempt to fill rooms with special lower rates and free meal deals. Spend some time with the yellow pages and weekend newspaper travel and entertainment sections to scout out best prices and special coupons. Put this information in your Special Fridays file.

Lend An Ear

Music is powerful — it can excite, get us dancing or marching or it can calm and soothe and erase cares. Search through your collection. Find the music that helps you let go and put it aside in your Special Fridays file. Go to the trouble of organizing cassettes or record albums of your favorites that get you in the calmest moods. Put these sources of restorative music away; don't overuse them. Save them for times of need.

Often you can find music appropriate for just such a Friday night in a New Age section of your nearby record store.

Dine In Style

Sometimes, after a demanding week, the thought of going home only to have to cook is a major depressant. One alternative can seem tasteless and sterile — the frozen dinner or the visit to a fast food restaurant take-out window. Another is too energetic — going out to dinner, including reservations, driving, parking, ordering, tipping and sometimes being rushed by an impatient server.

Consider a gourmet catering service and have an especially fine meal delivered to your door. Some caterers will also provide servers if your budget can handle it. These caterers can prepare your favorites to order or can provide a menu of their own to choose from. This, too, can be a wonderful gift!

Go Soak Your Feet

Particularly relaxing after a day of walking and standing is a good hot foot soak. Some commercial gadgets are available for this but we think the bath detox formula in a large enough basin or pail will do fine. Add hot water from a thermos continually, to keep it warm enough.

Consult Your Higher Power

Friday night can be the perfect time to leave the world of work and enter the world of the spirit. Going to a prayer service at your church or temple and allowing peace to enter your soul by commencing with the higher power you believe in is one of mankind's oldest and most successful practices. It just has to be better than a visit to a shopping mall or settling down to pay the bills.

Many times people allow nonessential details to get in the way. Worrying about what to wear to your place of worship or criticizing the style or content of the sermon are two guaranteed ways to lose the benefit and purpose of going. Let yourself surrender to the experience. Open your heart to it. Refuse to engage in banter. Be fully present (don't make exciting plans for after the services.) Be still. Be there.

If you'd rather choose the less formally religious, meditation offers the potential for healing a wounded psyche. You may choose, or already be part of, an established meditative group such as TM or yoga or you may have read one of the many good books on meditation. Also a variety of guided meditation audio tapes are on the market and provide a good background for beginners. Setting aside Friday nights for a meditative experience can help clear away the toxins and tensions of your week. Try it!

Pamper Yourself

Beauty parlors and men's styling salons have something wonderful to offer — facials, manicures, shampoos, pedicures — in short, pampering. It's an intriguing experience to be waited on literally hand and foot.

A facial cleans the pores, relaxes the face muscles and calms the whole body. All of these body services are so delightful that people get hooked on them — but it's a positive addiction.

The trick here is to find places that will do these on Friday nights. Some places that ordinarily close will stay open for an additional fee. How about doing this as a quiet "party" with several close friends?

Listen To Some Literature

Several companies now offer a wide variety of old classics and current best-sellers recorded by professional voices on cassette tapes. Being read to can be profoundly relaxing. This is a no-effort way of curling up with a good book.

You'll have your choice of the companies that offer the whole book word-for-word and those which condense in varying amounts. Either way, you can keep current in your reading while lying back on your pillows, eyes closed.

Do Your Own Thing

As the press of our jobs and commitments increase, many of us forget our hobbies and interests. Closets fill with materials and equipment untouched for many months. Friday night is a good time to pull all those things out and bring them back into our lives. Knitting, baking, crossword puzzles, a wood shop project, silversmithing, arranging your collection — all can be so involving that, hours later, the daily cares seem far away and the job of accomplishment fills your heart.

Read To Each Other

You and your partner scout up some luscious short stories to read aloud. Start over dinner with wine and candles. Finish cuddled under covers, reading with full artistry of voice in tone and drama.

Fill Your Photo Albums

How many of us have pictures waiting to be placed in plastic covers? Sort the pictures together with your partner. Put them in the albums (it relieves the guilt we feel about undone tasks) and relive the experiences the photos illustrate. It's a great time for reminiscing!

Now that you've laid the groundwork, you're ready for Saturday night!

PART II

How To
Make Your
Saturday
Nights
Live

Saturday Night Live

Exciting and memorable Saturday nights are like live theater: They are dramatic, have action, props, scripts and players. They take place on some stage and have to be managed and directed.

Each of our 52 Saturday nights is divided into three segments.

First, there is *The Scene,* which tells you what's on the agenda, who's there and what's happening. It describes the action.

Next is *The Script.* This tells you how to set it up — what's needed to carry out this Saturday night's entertainment, the ingredients, the motivation, the intent and the elements necessary to make it work.

Finally, we offer *Curtain Calls.* This explores ways to wrap up the evening, variations on the theme, culminating experiences, suggestions for more Saturday nights like it and results to be expected from the current one.

It's up to you to cast each drama, and like some of the best directors you can jump on stage and take an active role as well.

Saturday night scenes to which you might invite children are marked with this symbol:

After reading our ideas, you're on your own. It's you and the people you invite to share the experience who will make it an evening to remember.

Have fun!

Saturday Night #1

You're The Band Leader

The Scene

Send invitations to friends and neighbors to come to your house and bring musical instruments. Tell them that they don't have to be professional musicians. With luck, you'll find some guitar and banjo players and someone who can play the piano with dexterity (you can borrow or rent an electronic keyboard, if necessary). But make it clear that your guests can — and should — bring homemade instruments, too.

The singing and playing starts with the first arrivals. From solos to sing-alongs, it's going to be a memorable, musical night.

The Script

Invite several people whom you know to have either musical instruments or talent or both. You'll want some people who are really good singers or song leaders, as well as just plain folks with a sense of fun. Print enough of your favorite songs so that everyone will have a copy. Round up a lot of instruments, including such homemade ones as kettles and spoons, combs and wax paper, vacuum cleaner tubes and, the old standby, an old-fashioned washtub for a bass drum. Perhaps you can find other cheap instruments, such as triangles, kazoos and nose flutes. (Yes, nose flutes: a good music store will have these 50-cent plastic devices that anyone — without a head cold — can play!)

Curtain Calls

Give the band a name and tape record several key pieces. Play it back for the group. Agree to meet a second time.

Have a monthly or yearly reunion of the band.

Have T-shirts with the name of the band made for everyone.

Meet next summer for a big picnic; try to get on the program of a bluegrass festival.

Saturday Night #2

Kids Like
To Sing, Too

The Scene

About a month after your first music night, the group meets again. After dinner at someone's house, the band, complete with a trunkload of instruments, goes to a children's hospital. Song sheets are passed out to kids in their beds, and the patients are asked to join in the playing and singing. Nurses, doctors and other hospital staff are encouraged to join in the musicfest. Group members also pay a bedside visit to each kid and distribute T-shirts.

On the ride home, everybody talks about the high points of the evening and the general good feeling of having "left the campground better than we found it." They also talk about taking the show next to a senior citizen's home, a prison, halfway house, etc.

The Script

Contact the hospital or social agency at which you'd like to entertain. Ask for the volunteer coordinator. This might have to be a Saturday or Sunday afternoon, depending on schedules and physical conditions of the children. Make sure your people will show up; kids' expectations are being raised and they ought not to be disappointed. Plan dinner beforehand — perhaps as pot luck to build group spirit. Check to see who is going to carry which instruments in which vehicles, and who's riding with whom. Carpooling will get the party feeling going on the way there.

Make sure you have enough instruments to share with the children at the hospital so that each one has something to play. Prepare music sheets. Invite children's parents and brothers and sisters if the hospital approves. Send press releases to newspapers, TV and radio stations; it might encourage others to do the same.

Curtain Calls

Tape record at least some of the songs that the group does, and play them for the children. Consider collecting donations from your group and bringing a gift of a cassette recorder for the children's ward to play your tape and any others.

Saturday Night #3

Scary
Bonfire Bash

The Scene

On a secluded lakefront, beach, or perhaps a beautiful river, you have organized a bonfire Saturday night, and for a couple of weeks in advance you have collected driftwood and timbers, and piled them up in a secret section of the shoreline. On the appointed night, everybody has gathered together, the fire is roaring, the food is served and you start the first ghost story. You make it juicily scary, so people have to sit close together to give each other comfort.

You've prompted some of the other invited people to get a story ready, too, and at some point in the evening you start a serial story, where you begin the first part, then someone else jumps in and makes up the second part, and everyone around the campfire contributes to the story.

The Script

Gather firewood. See whether fire regulations require a permit and prepare for a safe fire. Make sure that the land is public, or get whatever permission is necessary. Send the invitations out. Gather together a few good books of ghost stories. Make copies of special stories and keep them on hand if some people attending need a story they feel they can use.

Divide up tasks — someone responsible for the fire, another for drinks, another for food, for music, guitars, photocopying, etc. Print up invitations that have puns on bonfires or burning, or that have lots of ghost pictures.

Remind people what kind of clothes to bring, based on the weather. Get things to sit on — logs, benches, blankets, tarpaulins — since shorefront land is usually damp.

Curtain Calls

Form a linked-arm circle around the fire and sing campfire songs. Provide song sheets. Have buttons or T-shirts made: "I survived the Ghostbusters Party." Take a group photograph.

Saturday Night #4

Celebrities On The Spot

The Scene

People are all abuzz. They can't wait to meet the celebrity guest and begin the grilling. The guest, who has been warned and knows what to expect, has an unusual occupation. What will it be tonight? Camp counselor or rape crisis counselor? Disk jockey or horse jockey? It could be a masseuse, porno shop manager, deli store owner, chef, sexy lingerie shop manager, private eye, chauffeur or bank guard. The person is interviewed — seriously or humorously or both, depending on what's appropriate for the particular guest, and how responsive he or she is.

Each member of the group has been assigned the role of reporter from a different newspaper, news magazine, TV or radio station. They've seen lists of possible questions to ask. They have been given a rundown on the proclivities and bias (if any) of the particular news outlet that they're representing. For example, National Review will take a "cocked-eyebrow" viewpoint — strictly a conservative perspective. Its reporter will participate in William Buckley's challenging style. A mock Playboy reporter will focus on the erotic perspective.

You are meeting someone who is outside your ordinary range of experience, getting a chance to talk on a deeper level than "Hot enough for you?" and "Did you see the Browns game?" Curiosity is awakened, and alternatives and choices in life are expanded.

The Script

Schedule your interview subject far enough in advance — with a guaranteed commitment to be there. Have a back-up person if the primary interviewee doesn't or cannot show. If you have to use the back-up person, an interesting thing would be to ask the questions prepared for your original guest even though they may not be appropriate. Or have a talented friend role-play the missing guest. Make a commitment to prepare stimulating questions. Ask some children to suggest questions. The invitation could be done in the form of a press release — "You're invited to a press conference to represent _____ " (blank space for what their media assignment is), and day, time, and name of person to be interviewed. Suggest sample questions, sources for advance reading on the subject and people to call to key in to controversies and issues worth exploring. Include a map with directions to the host's house.

Get your interviewee to the party on time: Send a good map and set of directions or, better yet, pick up your guest personally. Make sure to confirm at least a week before *and* the day of the event. Invite the guest to dinner at your host's. It may be necessary, in some cases, to pay an honorarium to the guest; each person attending would help pay the cost, split equally.

Curtain Calls

Interviewee leaves about 10 P.M. giving time for a group discussion: What did we learn? How did we feel about some of his or her answers? What would our answers have been to some of the questions? What were we most surprised or confused by? Would we want our son or daughter to pursue that career? What steps did the person take to begin that career?

Videotape or audiotape the interviews. Review all of the tape or sections of it when the interviewee leaves. Or review the tape with the subject present. Break up into groups of threes and fours, allowing more people to talk in a given period of time and encouraging shyer people to participate. Give each group a paper with questions like these:

- What was said that was most intriguing/interesting/memorable for you?
- What question was not asked — or answered — that should have been?
- What question would you have answered differently?
- What surprised you? What did you learn?

A final question to all: Who else would you like to interview?

Saturday Night #5

Full Moon Hike

The Scene

The invitation says, "Gather at our house on the night of the full moon and we will take a magic walk to the top of _____ (mountain or hill)." What a thrill it is when everybody gathers at the top and looks out over the valley and marvels at the landscape illuminated by the full moon. If no hills are available, a seashore or lakeshore will do as well.

Sit close together and think your thoughts silently for at least 15 minutes (try for more — and ask for that silence, in advance, clearly and firmly), experiencing what it feels like to be in and looking out on the universe. After the time of silence, you sit in a circle and tell one another of different precious thoughts and feelings you might have had on other mountaintops or when viewing any horizon. In that way you reveal yourselves to one another, making the intimacy grow by your sharing.

We want to encourage you to remember that there are many kinds of mountains we climb in our lives. Some are internal; some are in our relationships with self or with others. The "mountain" can be a metaphor.

The Script

Most state park trails are identified by white blaze markings on the trees so that by the light of the moon you can easily get up a mountain. To be sure, you can also go there earlier and tie bright reflective ribbons on trees to mark the trail. Get invitations out promptly. Make sure people arrive on time with hiking boots, if appropriate. Check in advance to be sure that the mountain, seashore or lakeside park is not closed at night.

Each person can take a little pack of snacks to eat at the top (and a trash bag so that you leave the place clean). Or ask each person to make a pack for someone else — and trade. Wear clothing appropriate for the place and time of year.

Curtain Calls

Share stories of other views participants have seen. Discuss other examples of nature's treasures that could be shared on future Saturday nights or Sunday afternoons. Invite someone from the Sierra Club or other outdoor group to accompany you and talk about hiking, camping and climbing activities throughout the year.

Saturday Night #6

Share A Sunset

The Scene

An ancient Japanese saying is that if you really like someone, you will invite them to share with you one of life's crowning experiences — a sunset.

Each sunset is totally unlike any other; each has its own special artistic and spiritual qualities, moods, colors and feelings.

You know a place where the sunsets are usually spectacular. So that's where you've invited your friends. When they arrive, you welcome them, give them some refreshment, discuss the setting and then, at the proper moment, you say: "It's time for us to share the sunset. And, please, sharing it is done silently." Your friends sit, wrapped in their own thoughts, perhaps hugging, perhaps sitting alone, sharing something that can't be put into words.

When the sun is fully down, and the last colors are fading from the sky, you all have more refreshments, some quiet talk, and perhaps a reading of poetry you've chosen for the event. Lovingly, the evening ends.

You may want to bring a good portable cassette stereo and play classical or contemplative music just after the period of silence — and before the talk commences.

The Script

Find a really nice locale where the view is not broken up by ugly manmade wiring, telephone poles and smokestacks. Shores of lakes, rivers and oceans are good for this; tops of hills are fine. Forests are also good, if there is a clearing, and places where there are rocks, to see the shadows cross. Don't overlook the vistas of big cities, either, watching the shadows move across the buildings. Finding a particular part of the city that is most picturesque is your job as the host or hostess.

Set up the location as you would for a very special picnic; taking care to provide some good blankets or tarpaulins, some flowers, some wine or soda and cheese, comfortable places to sit, floor cushions or beach chairs, a chaise longue or low-to-the-ground sand chairs. Bring blankets against the night chill and be sure to have flashlights. It might help to bring a couple of hibachis to radiate some heat and to enjoy the glow of coals as the dark approaches.

You might even choose to have a Japanese motif and serve warmed Japanese plum wine. Supply some non-crunchy (quiet) snacks.

It is important to keep this experience "pure" — not to let talk of business, news, sports, children or problems intrude. This should be made clear to your guests. Let them know what to expect. Unexplained rules of behavior often lead to disappointments and spoiled evenings.

Plan carefully for all the help you will need to bring the materials from the cars to your site — and back in the dark.

Curtain Calls

You might like to have a slumber party, where all get together and have some fun early in the evening, go to bed early, get up in the wee hours and go to the same location and share a sunrise. This could be followed by some exercise to music to welcome the sun. You might invite (or hire) a Tai Chi teacher to teach and lead. This is especially nice to uplifting classical music. End by cooking an outdoor breakfast, singing songs of joy, awakening and perhaps beginning the day with prayer.

Saturday Night #7

Santa's Helpers

The Scene

About a month or two before Christmas/Hanukkah, a group of handy friends comes together. The host for the evening has a certain number of simple wood-working tools — power saws, drills, hammers, wood-carving knives, screwdrivers, maybe a good jigsaw or bandsaw. The host has also found a lot of scrap wood and stockpiled it, and the guests have done the same. Everybody meets in the workshop and begins to design and put together things to give to little kids who don't expect much this season. Some examples: A ring toss made from broom handles stuck in boards, rope made into tossing rings, sets of blocks with pictures glued on the sides. The group takes a huge bagful of handmade toys to an orphanage, children's hospital or another appropriate place.

The Script

You'll want to collect materials for a considerable length of time. Ask neighbors and friends for materials; tell them you're planning to make toys for poor children. Visit clothing factories for cloth and leather. Go to carpentry shops and industrial lumberyards for free wood scraps — and ideas. Use the yellow pages. Get inexpensive paints and lacquers if you can, but make sure they are not lead based. Gather lots of nails, glue, screws and other hardware.

Go to a library and take out books on simple toy projects. Pick some simple projects from the books and copy just those projects so people don't waste the whole evening choosing one. Make a sample of each toy in advance. Invite everyone to bring their own tools. Divide up the labor — some people to saw, some to nail, glue, paint and so on. Try a team project approach. Package each toy when done. This can be a two-Saturday night event, one for making and painting, and the next for sorting and packaging.

Curtain Calls

A Sunday afternoon should be planned as Toy Delivery Day. The invitations could be printed in a toy theme. You've set it up with the orphanage, hospital, retarded children's home or other agency and worked out all the details so there'll be a minimum of disruptions and maximum delight as you arrive bearing these lovingly made presents.

As a follow-up, contact the occupational therapy department of a hospital and ask if there are any simple devices or games they might need. There are a number of things like wooden tic-tac-toe sets that therapists use to increase manual dexterity with inpatients who have had some kind of stroke or flexibility loss. Your party could make them as another Saturday night project.

Saturday Night #8

Comedians' Night Out

The Scene

Everybody brings their favorite stand-up comedy routines on record or tape to the party. The purpose: To share the artists you've loved down through the years.

The laughter soars as everyone sits back and listens to Mel Brooks' and Carl Reiner's "2000 Year Old Man" routine.

More hilarity follows excerpts from Richard Pryor's best albums. Bill Cosby and his special magic thrill the room. Everyone shares what has been truly precious to them in the world of stand-up comedy.

The Script

Everybody is asked to go through their collections and bring the ones they are most anxious to share, and with favorite segments set to play. Make sure you have a good cassette player and turntable so that people are not straining to hear the words. Alternate from one comedian to another to keep variety, freshness and interest high. Avoid listening to a whole album (of anyone) all at one time.

Curtain Calls

List all the comedians played that night and ask the guests to rank them in terms of which one was the funniest or most irreverent, or which most helped you regain perspective when things in life get too serious. Try to come to a group consensus without anyone having to "surrender" to group pressure.

Make a cassette recording of appreciation statements for the winning comedian and send it to him or her. People who bring that kind of pleasure really ought to be validated more often and more clearly. Applause alone may not be enough.

Make a master tape containing excerpts from a number of different comedy sources; it is especially fun to do it by theme. For example, five different comedians telling a mother joke or camel joke or political joke — because staying on a theme builds laughter and the "readiness to laugh."

Have clusters of people in each corner of the living room put together an original comedy routine based on one of the themes you've just heard.

Saturday Night #9

Concert In Your Living Room

The Scene

You have hired some talented local musicians to come to your home to play for your friends. A folk singer or a small jazz trio or perhaps a chamber music quartet. Your friends gather around and listen with respect and delight, and mingle with the musicians during intermission and at the close.

The Script

Move furniture to separate the audience and the performers. Turn off the telephone and minimize the possibility of other interruptions.

You can ask your friends to help with the expense by chipping in equal shares. One way to keep costs down is to hire student musicians. Many schools, universities and conservatories have excellent groups that charge a modest fee or perform for expenses only.

Sometimes musicians booked for a performance for a large audience, who have their travel expenses already met, will agree to appear for less money at a smaller event before or after, if scheduling permits. Check newspapers for coming concerts.

Ask your friends in advance for some musical requests and then ask the musicians to be prepared to honor them.

Think carefully about refreshments for the evening; make them blend with the theme of the music. For example, folk music might suggest down-home food; chamber music may mean imported cheese and wine.

Make sure payment is handled unobtrusively, either in advance or at the end of the evening in an envelope, not publicly. The musicians should be made to feel that they are invited guests, rather than merely paid performers. If you get a musician who has a record out, ask him or her to bring copies of the record. The group could buy one *in advance* for every couple who attends.

Curtain Calls

Have an after-concert coffee and cake session with musicians and guests. Encourage *small group* discussions about what it's like to be a musician; your favorite pieces; the sides of a musician's life the public never sees, etc.

If it is a chamber music group, you might want to have everyone dress in tuxedo and formals, and give everyone a libretto. If folk singers, have lyrics available and ask the musicians in advance if they'd mind having a sing-along as part of the evening.

Saturday Night #10

Protect Yourself

The Scene

At someone's home or at a dojo, you and your friends meet for an introduction to self-defense. Everyone is wearing casual, loose-fitting clothes. A professional instructor takes them through a few sequences in warding off attacks. They are taught some basic strategies that they'll be able to practice at home.

In addition to physical expertise, the instructor has been picked because of his/her knowledge of nonviolent techniques and of psychological methods of avoiding the use of self-defense.

The Script

Choosing a suitable self-defense instructor is the key to a successful evening. Some instructors revel in violence, and may in fact have enormous pent-up hostility. It is important, therefore, to pick someone who has a good perspective about the art of self-defense and will not make the evening a "heavy" one.

Also, be aware that your guests will have varying levels of physical ability, flexibility and endurance. Verify that the instructor will cooperate in making sure no one will be hurt or asked to do more than is comfortable. If you hear the instructor say, "No pain, no gain," you've got the wrong person. Guests should be reminded that whatever they do is their own responsibility and that the organizers assume no liability. In fact, it would be wise to ask participants to sign a disclaimer.

Curtain Calls

Show excerpts from some Bruce Lee movies or other martial arts films. Have fun parodying the dialogue.

At the end of the evening, you have a chance to accentuate the positive. Refreshments should include healthy foods, fruit juices, energy and endurance builders. Avoid stimulants.

This could be a prelude to other instructional evenings — roller skating, macramé, income tax preparation, guitar playing and so on.

Saturday Night #11

Alternative Desserts

The Scene

First, dinner is served. Then, when everyone has had almost, but not quite, enough to eat, each person presents a favorite dessert to be shared. You've challenged them in advance to create a truly healthy alternative treat. For example, our favorite compote is made up of stewed fruits, nuts, coconut, yogurt and honey in a mixture we call Nirvana, an alternative for all seasons.

People at the dinner are encouraged to talk about their experiences and struggles, if any, in bringing better nutrition to their families in an inviting way.

The Script

In the invitation, suggest some things you've done, or wanted to do, to enhance your family's meals. Ask for suggestions. And include a list of three or four cook-books with good dessert ideas, providing names and addresses of local health-food stores.

There are two ways for people to share their concoc-tions. One is for everyone to bring their dessert pre-pared, ready to serve. The other is to make the dessert at the party, but for this you'll need a huge kitchen and plenty of time. If cooking is to be done on the premis-es, ask guests to bring their own bowls, mixers and other utensils.

Another alternative is to ask a local cooking instruc-tor (the adult education department of the local school system may be able to help) and invite him or her to present a program on alternative desserts.

Curtain Calls

Everyone brings at least five copies of the recipe from which their dessert has been made. That way, guests get to go home with a handful of alternative recipes and new strategies for snacking and desserting without self-destruction.

Desserts are just one idea for such an evening. Next time, try creative soups, main dishes or salads. Why not spend an evening planning creative food to take on a journey? (Think about all the past munching on dubious foods in the car and stopping at junk-food restaurants on vacation trips.)

Saturday Night #12

Cheese And Verses

The Scene

Your guests were asked to bring three to five of their favorite poems and their favorite fondue. The poetry should not have any limits (even limericks will do), and the type of fondue (cheese, meat, vegetable, chocolate) should be chosen by the guest. They should bring fondue equipment too, if they have it. This is a fondue buffet of sorts, mixed with verses. In the background, some fine music is softly playing. Several guests are reading poems in between mouthfuls.

The Script

Make sure fondue cooking equipment is available. Provide suggestions to guests who have difficulty finding poetry or recipes. Check to see if anyone is allergic to any of the foods involved or if they clash with religious beliefs. Be sensitive to vegetarian needs. Provide enough alternatives so there'll be something for everyone. Ask guests to bring enough for themselves and one more.

Alternate fondue tasting with poetry reading. Give in to the temptation to read poetry about cheese, food in general, good taste or savoring life's special moments.

It should be an economical evening, since guests are bringing much of the food and entertainment themselves.

Curtain Calls

Other attractive combinations: Wine with music; barbecue with square dancing; cheese tasting in an art gallery.

Saturday Night #13

Meet Your Hometown

The Scene

There's much about your community that you haven't experienced. Why not explore? Go with friends to an airport control tower; watch the planes and listen to the conversations between cockpit and tower. Or go to night court. Or go to the waiting room at the jail. Join a food-stamp line. Visit a public health clinic. Become aware of the realities of life for some people who haven't had your advantages. Don't go as voyeurs, but as caring people willing to expand their horizons.

The Script

Call ahead to establish times of operation, get permission to attend, ask about appropriate attire. Find out how many observers are allowed at one time. This will save time and avoid disappointment. Make sure everyone knows what they'll see and the behavior expected of them.

Many large businesses welcome groups for tours conducted by knowledgeable leaders. Wineries are fun. Manufacturing plants can be fascinating. Newspaper production is exciting. They all encourage questions.

Curtain Calls

End with a processing session, designed to digest what the group saw and learned, how it will affect their future attitudes and so forth. It's also an opportunity to brainstorm for other places worth visiting.

Saturday Night #14

Sculpt An Evening

The Scene

You and your friends are watching a block of wood or stone come to life. You are visiting a sculptor in his or her studio. You have brought your own refreshments and are, of course, treating your host.

In gratitude for your interest, the artist gives you a "gallery tour," discussing style and meaning in the work.

The Script

Ask the sculptor how many visitors can comfortably be accommodated, what the ground rules are and any areas of sensitivity that visitors should avoid discussing. Ask if it's possible to watch the artist at work.

Before the visit, duplicate some good, short, provocative articles on sculpture, including any published reviews of your artist's work. Send them to each guest ahead of time.

Curtain Calls

Meet after the session to share feelings and perceptions.

Plan a follow-up session of hands-on sculpting with easy and inexpensive materials. Invite an art teacher to help.

Arrange visits to other artists — a painter, potter, glassblower, stained-glass artist, silversmith, wood carver, interior decorator, architect.

Saturday Night #15

"Flakes" Greet The Flakes

The Scene

This one almost has to be impromptu. You've waited for the first snowfall of the year, and here it is. Everybody gathers and goes out to make tracks in the snow, not to mention angel wings and giant sculptures. Then they come back to your house and talk about the celebration of winter and what we can do to make this one unique and fulfilling.

The Script

Your guests will have to be the spontaneous kind. It's hard to predict the first snowfall, as any meteorologist will be glad to tell you. So guests have to be willing to alter plans at the last minute. Make hurried phone calls as weather reports turn into flakes.

Have some "snowy" music ready to play and some

recipes for mulled wine. Don't forget the firewood.

Curtain Calls

Plan a ski trip as a group. Have a similar party on the first really "spring-y" night; the blooming of a certain tree your locality is known for; the first day the roads open up after winter in your area.

Sunbelt people: Disregard all of the above, and be grateful!

Saturday Night #16

Fast Food Fete

The Scene

You and your friends are dressed in formal attire. Your tuxedos and formal gowns are gorgeous, if a bit out of place. Nevertheless, on your table is a lighted candelabra and bottles of wine (or grape juice if you prefer or if the restaurant's license doesn't permit alcohol). This is gourmet dining. Mozart is softly playing, the silverware gleams on the linen tablecloths. Other customers are staring. For this is Wendy's, McDonald's or any other handy fast-food restaurant.

Several formal toasts are made, all standing, glasses raised. An after-dinner speaker seriously spouts appropriate nonsense.

The Script

Select your most fun-loving friends, those willing to

take the risk of being silly in public.

For attire, you can substitute "tuxedo T-shirts" but the real thing is best for this particular kick.

You'll need to secure permission from the restaurant manager in advance. Remind the manager of the positive image building, advertising value of the event. You might even invite the local evening news team to film the fun.

Curtain Calls

Next time, try taking over a real gourmet French restaurant on a weekday night, guaranteeing the owners a minimum number of patrons choosing from a select menu at a fixed price. The owner might even provide a strolling musician.

Saturday Night #17

Rent-A-Picket

The Scene

Using completely blank signs (or ones saying "This Space For Rent"), you and your companions picket City Hall. The media arrive and you announce that you are an organization looking for a cause; have sign, will travel. Give us a cause, you say, and we'll espouse it. On this particular day, you're just demonstrating your ability to picket.

Several members of your group interview passersby and ask them what they should be promoting or denouncing. What wording should go on the blank signs? What needs to be done in this city?

The Script

Get an assembly or parade permit from the city. That's number one. Otherwise, you may wind up in jail.

Signs need not be expensive. Large cardboard boxes will provide the backing for some colorful poster-board sheets. The poles can be inexpensive wood sold for tomato stakes or such.

Curtain Calls

After picketing, retire to a group member's home and spend an evening talking about your connections to social activism of any kind — past or present. Have someone read aloud selections from Thoreau's "Civil Disobedience."

Let consensus decide an issue the group feels strongly about, then go out and make a public stand — for real this time. Learn firsthand what's it's like to fully exercise your right to free expression.

Saturday Night #18

Serenade The Symphony

The Scene

Your local symphony orchestra deserves a treat, as well as some recognition. Your group does this by serenading the symphony. Members arrive outside symphony hall wearing "tuxedo T-shirts" and carrying weird home-brew instruments like tom-toms, kazoos and combs with wax paper to play their version of various famous symphonic and operatic works.

The Script

Get a volume discount from the T-shirt store. Obtain a wild fright wig for the conductor and strange stick for the baton.

Bring folding chairs, set up just like an orchestra, and of course a box for the conductor to stand on. Instruct musicians to take their time tuning up.

Try to ensure a good-sized audience. Inviting the media may help.

Curtain Calls

Have refreshments on hand for intermission. No, not for the players, but for the audience. Sell them and donate the proceeds to the symphony or a related scholastic fund for music students.

If you insist on a shred of respectability, invite some of the real orchestra's musicians to watch or participate. They have a sense of humor, too. Or so we've been told.

For variation, stage an "Art Day" — with easels, fingerpaints, berets and smocks — in front of the art museum.

As an added attraction, assemble your kazoo orchestra in front of the local natural history museum and sing "Dem Bones, Dem Bones, Dem Dry Bones."

Saturday Night #19

Visiting Royalty

The Scene

You are having a party with six to eight couples. One couple dresses in Arabian costumes. The rest pretend they are in the retinue of the Middle Eastern royalty. Your restaurant reservations were made with that understanding. Everyone bows and shows obeisance to the "royal" guests, who speak in an Arabic-sounding tongue. Throughout the entire dinner the drama is played out, with the other couples translating for the "royal" couple to the waiter or waitress.

The Script

Go to a good costume rental company for this one. Authenticity is everything. See how long you can keep up the pretense. Avoid giggling or conspiratorial looks. Let the laughs be external and loud afterward! Get

some colorful foreign paper money for the visiting royalty to leave for the waiter as a tip. (But be sure to pay
the bill — and tip again — in U.S. currency.)

Curtain Calls

Laugh your way home. Take a camcorder along for
the memories. Don't start any international incidents.

Saturday Night #20

Clowning Around

The Scene

You and your friends have put on whiteface and some other colorful clown makeup and are cavorting through the streets of your favorite downtown area. You do street comedy and clowning, while giving out balloons and candy. Try to involve passersby in routines and games. You enjoy experimenting with whiteface and notice how liberative it is to frolic unrecognized.

The Script

Invite a real clown or mime to help with makeup and to discuss the art of clowning. There are schools of clowning and several books on the subject. Read a little to get in mind the "philosophy" of clowning.

Experiment with conventions and expectations for

behavior in public places. Go to dinner together in your makeup. Bring cameras. Rent or borrow a camcorder and record the event.

Curtain Calls

Analyze this. What feelings arose in you? What barriers and blocks do you have that the makeup helped you ignore for a while? Are there any lessons in this for your daily life? What were the funniest things that happened?

Plan a costume party in an unusual and public place.

Take your clown routines to a group of shut-ins.

If you work in the right kind of environment, ask your co-workers to join you in a day of work in clown makeup. Watch your clients, customers and fellow workers loosen up in response.

Saturday Night #21

What Makes Your Relationships Tick?

The Scene

This evening is for singles in search of successful relationships. Among your friends and acquaintances are at least three couples that most people would agree are secure and loving. They, of all people, could be called successful couples. The single men and women take the couples to dinner and spend the evening asking personal questions, trying to find out what makes a relationship work.

A risky undertaking, but possibly quite rewarding. It will undoubtedly stimulate strong feelings and could be very revealing — far more than any night at a singles bar.

The Script

Agree on a list of questions. For instance: What are your partner's most endearing qualities? What are your secrets of developing and maintaining a successful partnership? How do you deal with conflicts of values? The list could be endless, but try to keep it close to the heart.

Have questions written on slips of paper to be drawn from a bowl. Couples pick one at a time but can elect not to answer any question, just saying, "We pass on this one." Another couple can answer it if willing.

Keep the focus positive. The idea is to learn about successful relationships, not failures.

Curtain Calls

Singles can discuss their own successful relationships, discussing what worked for them, too. Focus on sweet moments.

Saturday Night #22

The Play's
The Thing

The Scene

You have invited six or seven people to a Saturday evening drama party. Everyone has a copy of a play that is to be read that night. Everyone takes a part. The lights are dimmed, you set the scene, and the play is read. At the end of Act I, everyone talks about the issues that were raised, the themes that touched them personally, and then they go into Act II.

The Script

Get the invitations out well in advance to the people you want to read particular parts that Saturday night. The second task is to pick up the number of copies of the play that you need. Many are available in paperback. We'd recommend any Neil Simon play, with parts for men and women of all ages. Some very dramatic one-act plays are also available in paperback and would work well.

The invitation would be enhanced by a theatrical theme like a playbill, but other than that, make it simple, clear, direct. Ask your guests to arrive in a simple costume — just really a suggestion of what that character might wear rather than something elaborate — and to bring some props from a list you supply.

Curtain Calls

When the play is over, sit around and discuss ways in which a role might be like our real life, and how certain themes in our life are portrayed in the play. What a nice once-a-month club this could be! After you've done this several times with the same or different groups of people, pick your favorite one, videotape it and show it at a different party.

Get some old radio scripts from a library or the archives at a local radio station. Stand up at a microphone; get various people in the party to be the sound-effects technicians, the audio engineers, the director.

Another variation is to take the play reading to a senior citizens home when you've polished your performance.

Saturday Night #23

Twenty Questions

The Scene

Your group is seated in a circle and someone starts asking questions. They ask two questions of the person to their left. For instance: "What was the scariest moment of your life?" "When did you come closest to death?" "What are the three most joyous moments you can remember?" "What are two things you're looking forward to in the next year of your life?"

The possibilities are endless, but each questioner can ask only two at a time. The player who answers the questions then asks two questions of the next person in the circle and so on.

The same questions may be asked, but variety is encouraged. This continues around the circle until it comes back to the first person, who then asks questions of the person to the right, and back around the

circle again. Questions can be focused on a theme —
relationships, sexuality, politics, death, money, happiness, life, leisure time, recreation, anything. We find a
potpourri often most exciting. In that process we all
really get to know one another. We also gain skill in
asking and being asked questions that have some sub-
stance rather than endless small talk which often
dominates parties.

The Script

Pick your couples with care. With whom do you feel
comfortable and trusting? For whom do you have
respect and the wish to be closer? Because questions
can get personal, there's some real risk-taking in this
party. It certainly doesn't have the flavor of most parties you've attended. Try to keep it gentle. It's very
good to have some lighter or even humorous questions
in store to keep the balance of comfort. An important
ground rule is that everyone has the right not to
answer any question.

Prepare a page of sample questions and give everyone a copy.

Curtain Calls

From the questions asked, the group selects the
ones they'd like three world leaders to answer, and
then guesses what their answers would be.

Variation: Have the couples bring their children. The children write questions on cards. The couples still do the answering. What a chance for everyone to grow! Our experience is that the children's questions are often tender and filled with "innocent wisdom."

Let's Get Technical

The Scene

The computer age has left a few of us behind. Quite a few, in fact. For that reason, we're having a computer party or, to be exact, a word-processing party. The group gathers around a computer in someone's house. Other computer owners are plugging theirs in too. Some word-processing programs are different from others and this gives everyone a chance to compare.

Participants get to write a letter or perhaps print out a "For Sale" sign. They learn the differences between word processing and regular typewriting. Most people are fascinated by the ability to edit their work as they go along.

It's fun for neophytes to learn how to give commands and see the machines carry them out. What a sense of power! Although some end up as confused as when they started, they can at least say they have done battle with this technology and survived! Others can boast that they have conquered their computer phobia.

The Script

Having at least two or three computers available is almost a necessity. Everyone should get a chance to participate — not just watch. It's more fun and you learn more easily.

An alternative is to find out if you can use the computer room at a local school, under the supervision of an instructor who could do more than guard the equipment — you might get some helpful instruction to boot!

You're liable to get even more cooperation from a local computer dealer, who should be more than glad to show off his wares to a group and give some operating tips.

Curtain Calls

Before the evening is up, everyone has had the chance to write a letter, either to a newspaper or a lawmaker, bestowing laurels or bringing to their attention a pet peeve or a political cause. That way, the evening does double duty.

Form a cooperative buying group and ask a local

computer dealer to sell your members equipment and software at quantity discounts.

Meet regularly and support one another's developing skills.

Join a local computer users support group.

Saturday Night #25

Commercials You Love To Hate

The Scene

To attend this get-together you had to prepare well in advance. You were asked to either audiotape or videotape the worst commercials on the air, and to bring two or three horrible examples on a cassette, ready to share.

The first half of the evening is spent hearing and viewing these commercials, hooting and hissing.

The second half is spent writing parodies of these commercials, using real products or making up bizarre products to advertise wildly.

The Script

Give your guests plenty of time to listen for the worst commercials and, of course, time to tape them.

Some people may need technical help in learning to

tape off the air. Share your expertise or ask others to lend a hand.

Curtain Calls

Ask the group to write some commercials that make sense and do good. The wife whose husband has a headache doesn't simply hand him a pill, for instance, but talks about improving communication in their relationship and finding the cause of his stress.

Or how about a commercial for creative moments of silence? Sponsored, of course, by your local library.

Saturday Night #26

It's An Emergency!

The Scene

You're at the emergency ward of your local hospital. You keep hearing sirens. Every few minutes, an ambulance pulls up and orderlies unload another bleeding or comatose patient. Fortunately, you're only watching. You and the other members of your group have come here to broaden your outlook.

You sit or stand out of the way, quietly observing the orderlies, nurses and doctors rushing about, caring for the sick and injured. You find out what kinds of things happen in a city hospital on a Saturday night, and you notice that most of the victims are poor and powerless.

Then the group adjourns to someone's home and talks about what surprised them, what they'd like to see changed, and how they might accomplish that.

The Script

You arrange to go as a group and, while there, stay in a tight-knit, unobtrusive group. You will have to have approval from the hospital management, of course, to accommodate a group of observers. Have a preliminary meeting where you talk about appropriate behavior and your goals.

Curtain Calls

Use your new knowledge to help the hospital, either monetarily or as volunteers. Write to the hospital board of directors or appropriate political leaders to bring about any changes you think would improve the system.

Saturday Night #27

Christmas Craziness

The Scene

No one is unaware that the commercialization of Christmas has gotten out of hand. Every family has felt the pressures of giving and receiving gifts that aren't needed, which is the impetus of a Saturday night devoted to doing something to change attitudes.

On the theory that "change has to begin with me," a group of friends gets together in October (when the first jingles and Christmas sales usually begin) or November to talk about how the commercialization of Christmas is affecting their families. They talk about how they hate to have their children growing up in an environment that encourages a "buy me, get me, give me" attitude. They discuss alternatives and ways to introduce kids to gifts of service, love, time and connection.

The group produces a list of about 50 things that could be lovingly given to people; none of them have a price tag or require waiting in line at a cash register or checkout counter.

Participants are urged to recall what they received last year that they haven't used, and to give these to people who probably need them more.

The Script

Find magazine and newspaper articles in the library about the commercialization of Christmas and copy some of the best ones to send, with your invitation, to your guests.

Curtain Calls

Determine to give gifts of time, talent and energy.

Put on a multi-family garage sale to raise money for the truly needy.

Organize volunteers to donate their efforts in service to others.

Saturday Night #28

Collage College

The Scene

What do you mean you're not an artist? Have you ever seen the works of Robert Rauschenberg? His collages — bits and pieces of photos and drawings and everyday stuff — make millions. You may not have his talent for arranging things, but you can do collages, too. That's why you're knocking on the door of a friend's house with a pair of scissors in your hand and a stack of old magazines under your arm. You and the other guests are here to cut, paste and scotch-tape scenes for several collages.

You can work alone or with your partner and other guests, gluing the various elements on art cardboard. Best to stick to a theme, though, such as "Friendship," "Happiness" or "Goals."

The Script

Pretty simple. Just bring together people with disposable photos, magazines, newspapers, ads, brochures, fabric swatches, rug samples, labels, splinters of wood, and flotsam from dresser drawers and glove compartments.

Curtain Calls

The idea is to have an art show and sale to benefit a local charity. But first you need to hold other Saturday night events, dedicated to activities such as fingerpainting, clay and papier-mâché sculpture, cardboard-box sculpture and so on. Then you can have your art show.

Saturday Night #29

Eating On A Welfare Mom's Budget

The Scene

Friends — particularly friends whom you've had to dinner before — have been invited for a meal that is prepared on no more money than a welfare mother would have for a Saturday evening meal. The meal is simple, very starchy and certainly inexpensive. We talk about what our lives would be like if we had to live on a welfare budget. We talk about when (or if) we've known poverty. We talk about how we can help people who are poor, and we deal with the issue of how people with plenty treat those who have so little.

The Script

Some library research and, perhaps, some calls to

welfare and charity organizations, such as the hunger task force, will provide the information we need.

Curtain Calls

Check the yellow pages and various resource books and compile a list of charities to support. Research and try the diets of peasants in China, Africa or the Middle East.

Saturday Night #30

Just Joking Around

The Scene

Your guests have been advised to do their "humor homework." They have asked their friends and colleagues for their best jokes — jotting down notes or tape recording them — and have gone to the library for joke books. One at a time, the guests tell their favorite jokes, and the evening is filled with spontaneous laughter.

The Script

Send out a list of ideas for finding good jokes. A microphone on a stand would help turn this into a home comedy club.

Curtain Calls

Put together a little booklet of the best jokes and

sell them to benefit some charity. For example, you could use the favorite jokes of your neighborhood or your church's favorite humor.

Move the party to a local comedy club and invite young aspiring comics to start or end the evening (and steal some of your best material).

Saturday Night #31

Cop For A Night

The Scene

You are riding in the back of a police cruiser on a typical Saturday night looking for burglars, drunk drivers, dope dealers and all the other law violators police encounter routinely. Other couples are in other police cars. Afterwards, over coffee, your group talks about the crime situation, criminals and the criminal justice system.

The Script

This must be arranged with the police department well in advance. You may be able to get permission for only one couple, or one person, to ride — who will then report on the evening's events to the rest of the group. In some communities this is done frequently, and the police's "guests" are called "ride-alongs."

Curtain Calls

Invite police officers to a follow-up get-together and interview them. Do they find themselves getting hardened? How has it changed their lives? How do they see themselves as different from civilians? In what ways can individuals support the police or reduce crime?

Variations: Visit the fire department, the emergency squad, auto wreckers, Coast Guard, marine safety power squadrons, Civil Air Patrol.

Saturday Night #32

What's It Worth To You?

The Scene

Tonight's group is seeking to clarify values. For instance, guests are asked to list 13 things they use regularly that require electricity. You mean my hairdryer? Sure, your hairdryer. You mean my blender? Blend away, baby. Thirteen things that you use regularly and have to plug into a socket to make them work.

Some list a computer or electric typewriter, a tape recorder, radio, TV, stereo — the list lengthens quickly.

Next, guests are asked to remove five items from the list. And now they circle the five that they would keep to the bitter end. Everybody does that, and they laugh and talk about why they are saving the ones they save.

Now they're told there's a major national electricity

shortage, and you're only allowed to keep one. One of your top five. Which one will it be and why?

People do that and talk about why. What does it say about what we value? What does it say about where we are headed with our lives? Do we perhaps carry some useless baggage on our journey through life?

There is no right or wrong answer on what people keep, but in the process of the thinking and the sorting out, people get a chance to look at their values.

The Script

After the invitations have gone out, this is a relatively simple evening. All you really need at your house is some paper and pens or pencils, and a values exercise source book such as *Meeting Yourself Halfway* and *The Values Clarification Handbook*. You can read the directions right out of the book. The preparation is to pick three or four exercises before the evening starts.

Curtain Calls

Invite everyone to come again in another month and make up more exercises. Everyone attending is becoming clearer about what he or she values, and what a Saturday night can be for.

Buy and play the board game *Scruples* because it offers ambiguous dilemmas on value-related topics.

Save a month's worth of advice columns such as

Dear Abby, Ask Ann Landers, Miss Manners. Read the letters aloud to your group and have each guest answer a letter and read it to the group. After all have read their answers, read the columnist's advice and discuss which were more appropriate.

Set up some moral dilemmas. Ask the group to offer its solutions — and have each person call parents or clergy for their answers to the same dilemma. Try to predict the responses they'll give.

Saturday Night #33

Paddling By The Light Of The Moon

The Scene

The moon is full, the river (or lake) is smooth and you and your friends are slicing through the water in a half dozen canoes. It's peaceful and exciting at the same time. Someone is plunking a guitar and singing breaks out. At the designated halfway point, canoers take to the shore for a moonlit picnic. Then it's back to the starting point and the waiting cars for the trip home. A romantic night to remember.

The Script

Reserve the canoes well in advance. A canoe livery won't likely stay open at night unless assured of a certain amount of business.

Have your picnic site designated and ready.

Have each couple bring a picnic basket — for someone else. And make sure someone brings a guitar or banjo. Let everyone know who's invited.

Don't select a stream with a fast-moving current, which would make the return trip difficult. Do make sure of life preservers and be aware of the on-the-water experience or inexperience of the people invited.

Curtain Calls

Next, try a raft trip by the light of the full moon. Or a hike. Or a snow trek. There are lots of things to do with friends when the moon's out and the stars are bright.

Saturday Night #34

Knots To You!

The Scene

Here's an evening for crafty people who like to make lacy things with their hands. But your guests have been invited for a macramé evening without regard to their ability or technique. There'll be varying skills. Neophytes can team up with experienced people, and everybody will make a simple project. It's a chance for learners and teachers to benefit from each other. At the end of the evening, everyone will have learned basic knots and will take home pieces they have made. It's the kind of party made for all ages, from grandmas to kids.

The Script

The invitation reads: "Why knot come to this party? Come and make macramé with friends, enjoy the excitement of tying one on — without alcohol!"

Hosts need to round up different kinds of yarn and string plus a small assortment of spring clips for beginners to handle the knots. Pick up a macramé idea book. Ask macramé veterans to bring some of their yarn and ideas. Ask everybody to bring whatever snacks they want — you'll provide the beverages. Stress the idea that they can bring children and other relatives.

Curtain Calls

Other handy evenings: knitting, embroidery, latch-hooking, etc. Be on the lookout for acquaintances with a variety of craft skills.

Saturday Night #35

Just A Thought

The Scene

Your guests have brought newspaper and magazine clippings and books with highlighted passages — short excerpts from a novel, a couple of pages from a play, selected poems, an essay, a motivational book. The only requirement is that they be inspirational. For that's the kind of evening this is. Everyone gets to read something — as long as it's inspirational, moving, hopeful, positive and growth-provoking. Hopefully, each guest has 10 to 20 minutes worth of exciting reading.

When the readings are done, the group can discuss them and copies can be exchanged. It's a fulfilling evening of close friends expanding their horizons by sharing intimate thoughts.

The Scripts

A few phone calls in advance to set it up, specify what kind of material you're looking for, then reminders on the day of the get-together should do it.

Curtain Calls

Readings are nice any time. So are tapes. Next time, inspirational tapes can take center stage — featuring such speakers as Norman Cousins, Jack Canfield, Zig Ziglar and Denis Waitley.

Saturday Night #36

DJ's In PJ's

The Scene

Guests bring their favorite records of long ago —
LPs, 45s, tapes — whatever they have of the music
that meant a lot to them when they were in their
teens, when they might have had pajama parties.
That's what this one is. Each person gets a chance to
play his or her favorite cuts. There are bound to be
sighs, laughter and impulsive dancing! Sometimes the
gang will join in a chorus and everybody will sing their
hearts out. It's a chance to remember, reminisce and
rejoice in sweet thoughts from the past. And to hear
the music that was so important once upon a time.

The Script

The invitation asks that guests not only bring their
favorite albums from the distant past, but also plan
exactly which selections they'll play.

Include the addresses and phone numbers of recycled record stores, in case anyone wants to hear a song they don't have recorded.

Curtain Calls

Try to find some of the people associated in your mind with the music. Ask around, check school and courthouse records, see if there has been or will be a school reunion. They might like to know you still remember them.

Saturday Night #37

All Alone

The Scene

Once in a while you need a Saturday night to yourself. You bid a loving and tender goodbye to your spouse and your kids and you are off on a solitary jaunt. Your spouse has an adventure planned, too. The kids are staying with friends or relatives, their own necessary time away from parents.

No matter how close you are, there are times when spouses need a break. Perhaps you differ on which play or movie to see, or one wants to play racquetball and the other just wants to visit friends. Why not some creative or casual time apart to help you both appreciate your time together?

The Script

It's important to discuss this thoroughly so it's clear that no message of rejection is either being sent or received.

Make sure you both really agree on this one and that it isn't just one person's idea being rammed through against the other's wishes.

Be clear on when you'll both be back, so neither of you has to worry. Then spend time together sharing the results of your separate evenings.

Curtain Calls

If you have more than one child, periodically arrange for a "mommy-alone-time" with one and a "daddy-alone-time" with another. Kids enjoy the undivided attention of one parent for an evening.

Saturday Night #38

This Ain't Zoning, Folks

The Scene

This is a follow-up on the values exercise in Saturday Night #32 — What It's Worth To You. Planning boards help you to rank values by priority. These boards aren't like those planning and zoning boards appointed by city councils to decide what shops can go where. But they do help you decide what values go where. The boards themselves are shirt cardboards or big sheets of paper — anything to give you room to juggle 12 ideas on the subject you have chosen and let everyone take a look.

Your group can spend this Saturday night pondering how you can have more love and less conflict in your families. The host passes out the planning boards, on which are two columns of numbers in six rows, 1 to 6 on the lefthand side and 7 to 12 on the right. Guests are also given 12 slips of paper or cardboard on which to write ideas. These pieces will be moved around the board as the discussion proceeds. All ideas begin like this: "How valuable it would be to . . ."

Some possibilities:

1. Have a regular family discussion meeting each week.

2. Show approval at every opportunity and withhold criticism.

3. Have a weekly touch session in which one person at a time is lovingly patted by other family members.

4. Agree on a system for resolving conflicts.

5. Divide the household chores so that everyone takes part and no one feels overburdened.

6. Make time for family music get-togethers — playing instruments and/or singing.

7. Economize so that you can finance a mini-vacation once a month for the whole family.

8. Keep a family history, take lots of family photos and review them regularly for progress.

9. Celebrate birthdays with gifts of time and attention, validating the celebrant's unique talents and place in life.

10. Have a creativity night, when family members present an idea, an artsy-craftsy creation, a poem, a song, a dance.

11. Develop, possibly over a period of months, a set of family values that everyone agrees to abide by.

12. Make it a point to overlook mistakes and foibles, giving each family member the right to be wrong.

As the group discusses the dynamics of each idea — and each one's impact on the other ideas — individuals move them up and down the scale as priorities change.

The Script

The host draws up the planning boards, cuts the slips of paper for ideas and prepares an explanation of how it works. From there, it pretty much runs on its own. Add refreshments, of course.

Curtain Calls

The possibilities of planning boards are limitless. They provide the framework for dozens of fruitful Saturday nights.

Saturday Night #39

Caroling The Commuter Train

The Scene

This one is best reserved for suburbanites who live close to a commuter railroad station. Families gather at the station, children included, and sing Christmas carols as the 7:15 or 8:37 pulls in. The train stays in the station for about five minutes so that passengers who aren't getting off can enjoy the tunes, too. Afterwards, the carolers adjourn to the organizer's home for hot cider and some more singing.

The Script

You need to write to the railroad company and ask if they will delay the train an extra five minutes at such-and-such a stop for this night only. A follow-up phone call the day of the event will help to make sure the conductor knows to delay the train.

The group is supplied with song sheets and candles (or flashlights made to look like candles), and later with cold-weather refreshments. All carolers can supply their own mufflers and woolen caps.

Curtain Calls

You can do the same thing at an airport terminal or a cross-country bus depot. At the airport, though, only deplaning passengers and those waiting to board other flights will be able to hear the singing, of course.

Saturday Night #40

Matchmaking Couples

The Scene

This is a party for mixed singles and doubles, and we're not talking about tennis. The couples are here to do some matchmaking, or at least to make their experience available to curious singles, who make up about half the party. The evening is devoted to exploring how relationships are put together.

Each couple comes prepared to describe their first three months together. They answer such questions as "Where and how did you meet?" or "How fast did the relationship develop?" or "How soon did you go to bed together?" (if brave enough to say) or "Were there any bumps in the first three months?" or "How did previous relationships affect this one?"

The evening can follow a sort of script or the singles can ask their own questions. The singles should also talk about their own questions. They should talk about their own experiences, and possibly voice frustrations about the difficulty of finding the right person in this complex world.

The Script

To get things started, no special preparations are needed, except for refreshments and a list of reasonable questions to ask. Invitations and follow-up phone calls will help. An outline of typical questions might put the couples at ease.

Curtain Calls

Each single suggests another couple to talk to, as well as additional singles, if a second party is arranged.

Saturday Night #41

Saturday Night Special

The Scene

This Saturday night is for developing Saturday night ideas. It's for couples who get together a lot and have fallen into a rut of going out to dinner and maybe a movie. This night you have dinner at someone's house and talk about getting out of the rut. The evening is spent brainstorming the kind of ideas we've been discussing here. Ideas for doing something that might be more fun and less expensive. A facilitator might make suggestions and stress that the sillier the idea, the better and that people can piggyback on others' ideas. Quantity is what you're after — the more ideas, the merrier.

The Script

Just make sure you invite your more creative

friends, people who aren't afraid to speak up. It can be a potluck dinner if the host doesn't care to cook.

Curtain Calls

Another party will be needed to polish the original ideas and weed out the unworkable ones, or at least the ones that don't generate a lot of support. Then start planning the ones that do.

Saturday Night #42

Unbirthday Party

The Scene

All the guests are gathered at a long table, some dressed as Alice, some as the Mad Hatter and other characters from "Alice In Wonderland." A recording of "A Very Merry Unbirthday" from the Disney production is playing as the cake is brought out. It's no one's birthday — but everyone's unbirthday, and each person has brought a wrapped gift for someone else. Streamers, balloons and crepe paper festoon the room. Guests of all ages help to celebrate the free child in all of us.

The Script

You've made sure to invite only those whose birthdays do not fall on the date of this party. Get a recording of the Disney tune. Call a local costume rental shop to explore possibilities. The party will work with a small group, but the more people the jollier.

Guests are asked to bring one wrapped, beribboned gift. Specify a price range. You can have random gift giving or prepare people and let them know who their recipient is in advance; but A gives to B, and B to C and so on. It shouldn't be reciprocal.

Curtain Calls

Try a season birthday party four times a year. All friends and neighbors whose birthdays are in the spring, for instance, are invited. Next come the summer babies and so forth.

Saturday Night #43

Grandpa's Night

The Scene

Three or four families have gotten together to experience a Saturday night as our grandparents might have lived it when they were kids.

Thanks to Thomas Edison, there was electricity by that time, so the get-together doesn't have to depend on candlelight. And there was radio. But most of today's grandparents had only heard about television. It was all the rage at the time of the 1939 New York World's Fair, but it would be another decade or more before TV sets became common in American households.

So, in Grandpa style, our guests sit around and listen to tapes of old radio programs: "Fibber McGee And Molly," George Burns and Gracie Allen, the famous W. C. Fields and Charlie McCarthy debate, "I Love A

Mystery," "The Phantom." Spine-tingling mysteries,
stand-up comedy, soap operas, melodramas, family situation comedies — all these staples of modern TV got
their start on radio.

Older people at the party talk about other forms of
entertainment, how parties in the 1930s and 1940s
differed from those of today, and about the lack of modern conveniences that we now take for granted. The
group makes a list of such things as dishwashers,
microwave ovens, cassette recorders, fax machines and
other products that were developed long after our
grandparents were kids.

The Script

Invite whole families, especially those with grandparents at home who are especially welcome. Go to a
well-stocked record store and ask for tapes or records
of old-time radio shows, famous oratory, popular and
classical music and anything else you can think of. Do
some library research on what households were like
back in pre- and post-World War II days.

Curtain Calls

After listening to samples of this radio fare, the
group discusses ways that radio shows were superior
to television. (One way is that radio forced you to use
your imagination and drew you more personally into

the production.) What are some others?

Other discussions can center on materialism — do all of today's work-saving and entertaining gadgets really make life easier? Are we happier because of them?

Saturday Night #44

Looking For Roots

The Scene

With some of the same people who enjoyed Grandpa's Night, and others, the group does tape recorded interviews sessions with old-timers.

Each family's patriarch or matriarch is asked about experiences in childhood, what life was like back then, what they remember about their relatives, what stories they remember hearing from those who have passed on, and so forth. This could be the beginning of an oral history for each family involved.

The Script

Make sure the oldest members of the various families are urged to attend, and ask them to bring with them old pictures, family Bibles, marriage and birth records, mortgage notes and all kinds of other family records that might trigger memories. Make sure each family has its own tape recorder and plenty of tape. Video recordings are also great if available.

Curtain Calls

Follow-up taping sessions are probably inevitable. The families may want to appoint one of their own to begin an organized oral and written family history, collecting as much memorabilia as possible.

Saturday Night #45

Our Gratitude Is Showing

The Scene

Some of your best friends are here, especially those who are gracious, warm and thoughtful. But, for balance, some less outgoing and expressive people are at the party, too.

The object is to find out how much we have to be grateful for. So this is a brainstorming session. Each person in turn begins exploring all the things that help to make life wonderful — the people in your life, what they've done for you, what it has meant to you and so on.

The Script

You want to invite people who live productive, fulfilling lives and are grateful. But you also want people who may not realize how much they have received and how much they have to give. This can be a learning experience.

Curtain Calls

Now that we've counted and catalogued our blessings, it's only natural that we express our gratitude. Phone calls and letters are next on the agenda — to let all the people who have helped us on our journey know that we know the part they have played in our lives, how important they are to us and how much we appreciate them.

Saturday Night #46

Handyman's Special

The Scene

Everyone has arrived at the party with a piece of furniture that has seen better days. Every piece needs refinishing, and with everyone working together, helping each other, off comes the old flaked and scarred paint and stains. With shared power tools, chisels, techniques and advice, the old finishes are removed and new paint, stain or varnish is applied.

"Before and after" photos are taken, of course, and all guests are thanked for their contributions to each other's magnificent "new" furniture.

The Script

Make sure you have on hand or guests are bringing all the appropriate tools, stripper, paint remover and various finishes that will be needed. You'll need to find out beforehand what each person is bringing and what they have in mind. Everyone should bring rubber gloves and wear old clothes.

Have music prepared to play and, if one of the guests has the talent, someone to lead the singing. For, as everyone knows, work goes faster while you're singing. Make it a play night, not a drudgery night.

Curtain Calls

Other handyman jobs, such as electrical and plumbing projects, repairing locks, installing burglar alarm systems, etc., can be studied, if not actually undertaken, at the next party, and guests can share their knowledge and expertise.

Saturday Night #47

Childhood Tastes

The Scene

This is a dinner party to which everyone brings a dish of something that was terribly important to them as a child — something unforgettable that stirs childhood emotions. Maybe it's baked potatoes that have boiled carrots mashed into them, served by a tender, loving mother. Maybe it's pan-fried corn bread and turnip greens — your father's specialty. Maybe it's caramel-covered baked apples cooling on the kitchen windowsill. Everyone has some dish that was exquisitely delicious, one that, for whatever reasons, brings back fond memories.

As the guests share their dishes with each other, they talk about what they remember best and the culinary experiences that stick in their minds.

The Script

Let your guests know in advance that you want to recapture tender memories of your childhood through food, and ask each one to bring enough of their favorite childhood dish to share with the group. Each person should also be asked to bring along the recipe for others to try.

Curtain Calls

You might ask your own children about their favorite dishes and resolve to fix them more often.

Saturday Night #48

Master Builders

The Scene

Your family and two or three others with whom you are close (or want to be) gather in a recreation room. Your construction materials are boxes of flat toothpicks and popsicle sticks. Many small squeeze bottles of fast-drying glue are on hand, as well as newspaper spread on the floor.

The whole group picks a theme or goal and subdivides to complete the work in sections. The fantastic construction arises, first slowly — then picking up speed as sections that were separately assembled and glued are added to the whole.

It might be the Statue of Liberty, the Empire State Building, the Sears Tower, a tenement neighborhood, an abstract sculpture representing planet Earth. Whatever your theme, the group works together to build this work of art.

The Script

Involve everyone in buying, gathering and choosing the materials. The basics are lots of toothpicks and popsicle sticks. Cloth, felt, paint, wire, found objects, bits and pieces of household stuff are just fine, too. One nice idea is to invite everyone to rummage through a drawer at home and bring one personal object to contribute to the construction. Provide waxed paper — it's great for assembling sections to glue and dry on because nothing sticks to it.

Avoid perfectionism, put-downs or rejections of people's ideas. Be inclusive. Make the project big enough to include parts that, perhaps, do not fit one group's idea of the whole but satisfy another's. Strive for accepting and validating the contributions of all.

Photograph the project in varying stages of completion. You could even set up a video camera on a tripod in a corner with the lens on wide angle, and take a one-minute shot of the process every ten minutes for a "stop-motion" review of the growth of the project.

Curtain Calls

Sit back and glow with pride in your work and in having successfully collaborated with the other "sculptors."

Variation: allow the children to be the directors, foremen, organizers, delegators, planners, designers and architects, and have the adults be the willing and obedient construction workers.

Saturday Night #49

Counter Encounter

The Scene

This party is for the people around town who usually serve you. The young newlywed at the coffee shop who serves your eye-opener, for instance. And the college student who clerks part-time at the cleaners, the friendly proprietors of your neighborhood mom-and-pop grocery store, the jolly woman at the bakery who always saves you a fresh loaf of sourdough bread. You know, all those people you encounter day by day but never really get to know too well.

Here's your chance. Now you can get to know them as people and friends, and introduce them to each other. It's a great way of networking, of course, and of making friends.

The Script

Since you aren't exactly bosom buddies, and since

not everyone knows each other, keep everything light and casual. Take nothing for granted except the fact that you are among friends. Serve nonalcoholic drinks, some nice snacks and keep the conversation casual and not related to the individual's job. Instead of asking, "How did you get to be a hair stylist," for instance, ask them about places they've been or would like to visit. Talk about what you were like as children and how you've changed. "How did you meet your spouse?" is always a good opener, not to mention 20 great ways to spend a Saturday night or six things you bought that turned out to be a complete waste of money.

Curtain Calls

The night ends casually and cordially — perhaps with a little thank-you poem you've scratched out for the occasion (doggerel is okay) to each guest in his or her own envelope.

Saturday Night #50

Have A
Safe One

The Scene

This is strictly your own family affair. Everybody stays home tonight and helps make the house safer.

All of you go through the house evaluating it in terms of safety. Where are the fire hazards? Would this pile of clothes or those stacked-up boxes be a hazard if you had to get out quickly? Could you trip and fall here? Where are the fire extinguishers located? Do the doors have safety bolts? Are there toys or tools lying around that could cause an accident? What about sharp instruments or heavy objects improperly supported? Check outside: Is there anything a visitor could stumble over?

The family goes to bed and then, at a given signal, goes through an actual fire drill. It's fun, and it could save lives.

The Script

Check with fire and police departments — and your insurance company — for brochures and advice on how to make your house safer. Do library research. Then pick an evening when no one has any commitments and everyone agrees to stay home.

Curtain Calls

You'll all feel more secure knowing where everything is and what you need to do in case of an emergency. And you can brag to your friends. It might motivate them to be more safety conscious, too.

Saturday Night #51

Harry And Rosemary's Surprises

The Scene

This is one of our biggest favorites. We learned it from Harry and Rosemary Wong, our very good friends. They have a tradition of surprising each other every six weeks with a "mystery getaway." One time it's Harry's turn, next time it's Rosemary's.

It's your turn. Six weeks ago, it was your partner's turn. He or she took you to a wonderful place. You've been scheming, ever since, to create an even juicier surprise.

My wife Meladee planned this one for me: She told me we were going away. (Since it was our regular "six week Harry and Rosemary weekend," I had reserved the dates in my calendar.) She told me what kind of clothes to pack and for how many days. "Two nights," she said, "And nights can get cool there, so pack long sleeve shirts and take a sweater." She smiled. That's because sometimes we don't tell the truth. Sometimes we say, "Bring your mukluks, snowshoes and a croquet mallet." And those items have absolutely nothing to do with where we're going! This keeps the surprise factor high. You never know where you're going to be taken.

So I packed and, at the appointed hour, got in her car. We drove for what seemed to be endless hours. She changed directions several times so as to confuse me. She distracted me with an interesting story. Suddenly I knew that we were in the Sierra gold country, quite a distance from our home. "Where are we going?" I asked curiously. "None of your nevermind," she answered cheerily. "Come on, where are we going?" I asked again. She gave me six different answers, none that turned out to be true.

Four hours from our home, in the gathering evening, we pulled into a mountain ranch road and drove by pastures of llamas, beautiful and (mostly) gentle animals with variegated coats. Finally we drew up to a breathtakingly beautiful rustic multistory ranch house perched on a steep hillside. "We're here!" she exlaimed. "It's a working ranch that raises llamas and it's also a bed and breakfast inn. Are you happy?"

Now, it's easy to answer that kind of question. I was with the lady I love the most and away from phones, bills, kids, chores, responsibilities. I was in a pine forest at a beautiful retreat. Was I happy? You bet I was! We had two days of bliss before heading back to civilization. And the hot tub under the stars was indeed heaven.

The Script

Every six weeks one partner has to plan a surprise getaway. It can be just one night or one afternoon, a whole day or a whole weekend. But it has to be planned by only one partner and the other must be unaware of the plan.

You can take your partner to a restaurant you've never before visited (or you can choose a specially romantic one you've always loved). You can find a wondrous and fun activity you've never done before — like the dinner cruise on a sailboat that you can find in San Francisco Bay or the special steam locomotive train ride through the Cuyahoga Valley in Ohio.

Curtain Calls

Hunt through a good bookstore for the books that list bed and breakfast inns, and one-day trips in your locality (some TV stations produce these for free), and ask your automobile association for help in planning.

Ask your friends and colleagues for ideas: "What's the neatest place you've found within one day's drive from here? Have you got a secret place you've found that's specially scenic, pretty, restful and/or exciting?" You'll be surprised at the large number of suggestions you'll be given.

Most major newspapers have a "weekend" section and a travel section. Go through these regularly. When an unusual and exciting suggestion is published, cut it out and put it in your special Harry and Rosemary file. Even if you can't do it now, it might be an idea for next year.

Saturday Night #52

Suitcase Party

The Scene

On a particular Friday night, a bunch of people carrying overnight carry-on suitcases gather at the departure lounge of one airline at an airport. There are drinks and snacks; music is playing on one of those portable boom-box stereos. The mood is tense but convivial. Months before, each couple contributed money toward the "pot" for this party.

At a certain moment, a large bowl is produced in which there are slips of paper. On each is written the name of one of the couples attending. A stranger is asked to reach into the bowl and pull out the winning slip. When the name is announced, that couple is immediately awarded the prize. With applause, pats on the back and many hugs, they pick up their suitcases and are handed a travel packet that includes tickets to many weekend events in the big city! A city to be reached by a plane departing that very evening.

They have tickets for plays, an American Express coupon for dinner and all the trimmings at a fine restaurant. They are going to have a weekend, mostly expense-free, in an exciting city doing a lot of stimulating things. If it were New York, for example, they would go to a good hotel in Manhattan, have tickets to a Broadway play or two, a coupon for dinner at a fine restaurant and a map or guidebook telling them where all the good museums and other activities are. The entire group stages a grand bon voyage celebration at the gate. Streamers, whistles, hats, flash cameras with instant film, champagne!

As the winning couple flies off, the rest of the group leaves the airport in a convoy and drives to one of the homes or to a large party room, where the party continues so that everyone enjoys the evening while the winning couple enjoys the weekend.

The Script

This one is a big commitment. You should begin making all arrangements and amassing contributions at least four months in advance.

Curtain Calls

Some (or all) of your group meets the returning couple at the airport on Sunday, but they wait until the following weekend for a How-Did-Your-Weekend-Go? Party and to begin planning for the next Suitcase Party. Bring a video camera to the airport to interview them when they land. Behave as though they are celebrities; invite the media.

Variation: Rent a beautiful secluded cabin in the woods, or a penthouse suite at a fine hotel. Stock it with abundant and interesting food, wine, candles, delectables and supplies for a delightful party. The weekend begins with a whole-group party Friday night. All the couples assemble for fun and frolic. Halfway through the evening the slip of the winning couple is then pulled from the bowl. They get the cabin or suite for the rest of the weekend. The group continues the party and ends by cleaning up the cabin before they leave so the winning couple doesn't get stuck with the job.

PART III

Wonderfully
Sweet
Sunday
Afternoons

Sweet Sunday Afternoons

Some wonderful experiences are best saved for Sunday afternoons. There are lots of things you can't do at night, either because you need daylight or because they are just not appropriate for a Saturday night. Sunday afternoons, though, are perfect.

Here are a few ideas for making Sunday afternoons as memorable as your Saturday nights.

Turn Off The TV

Better yet, cut the cord. Just nip the plug off, so that the TV set is unusable for right now — yet you can restore it to service with a 79-cent repair. With the plug out of commission temporarily, you won't forget or lose your resolve and plug it back in. Why not leave it off for a few days? A few weeks?

See what it's like to be in the house when people can

actually talk to each other without having to shout or
repeat what was just said, or without having to turn
down the volume. What's more, you can actually come
up with your own ideas for things to do, things to
enjoy, rather than being sponges for someone else's
idea of entertainment.

To be meaningful, ideally the cord should be cut on
a football day.

Treasure Hunt

This is a simple activity for families. You invite several families to join you in a park, and each family is
given a list of what they have to find in the next half
hour. The list includes a fern, a piece of oak bark on
the ground, a beer can, ten beer can loops, a moss-cov-
ered rock, an acorn, a pinecone and a piece of dead poi-
son ivy. Of course, you have to have a few items that
are hard to find. People scatter in different directions
with plastic bags to put the loot in. When all come
back — they talk about the beauty of the woods and
how much fun it was to be there.

Neighborhood Benefit

Organize all the neighbors on the block for a neighborhood tag sale, also known as a garage sale or yard
sale, and use a certain percentage of the money raised
for some neighborhood improvement.

Family Fast

Spend a Sunday afternoon fasting. Donate the money you would normally spend on food as a gift to help relieve world hunger.

Arty Party

Get a set of inexpensive watercolors and some cheap watercolor paper, and go looking for something to paint. Everybody involved should have their own watercolors and pad of paper. Find a really beautiful location, maybe by the banks of a river or near a bridge or some beautiful valley, and spend the whole day painting the scenery.

As the light and color change, you make a second attempt, and a third and fourth if desired. No need to be perfect. Just try to capture what you feel about what you see in front of you. And develop some sense of the artist's struggle to convey that same feeling.

Follow up the painting with a little art show Sunday evening. Invite some friends over to view the family's production and to share some wine and cheese.

Season Sampler

Start in the spring or one of the other seasons and go to a nearby woods or park and collect samples of things representative of that season. Bring your cameras along. Go to a certain spot and have everyone take a picture of the view. Make a date to come back every three months and do exactly the same thing. Then compare and mount on a big board all of the pictures and samples of twigs, leaves, bushes, little plants and so on. Four seasons in one favorite spot. What a show!

Family Fun

Organize new activities for everybody in the neighborhood, giving people an opportunity to learn different things to do with their families. Organize it like a block party. For instance, on a day when it snows, organize a toboggan run. Get neighborhood families together for fun in the snow. In warmer climes, get friends and neighbors together for a group bicycle trip. Or a walk in the woods. Or an afternoon at the beach.

How Does Your Neighborhood Sound?

Take a portable cassette recorder, and you and the family make a sound picture of your neighborhood. Record the sounds of children playing, horns honking, dogs barking, church bells ringing, mothers calling their kids in from play — whatever life in your neighborhood is like on a Sunday afternoon!

Cousins Reunion

Organize a reunion of just your cousins. Don't let any of the aunts or uncles come — just the cousins of whatever age. This offbeat get-together can strengthen your family ties.

Barn Raising

If you see that a family is trying to build their own house or an addition in your neighborhood, round up other families and offer to be extra hod carriers and nailers and cleaner-uppers. Devote an afternoon to helping somebody build their house, and from then on every time you go by it you'll know that you are a part of that house.

Gardening On The House

On one Sunday, get your family together and all of your gardening implements, and go over to help a neighbor with lawn and yard work. Do all the work that they need and enjoy the pleasure of helping someone else.

Rent A Rink

Rent an ice rink or a roller rink. Invite all your friends and ask them to invite a friend. Fill the rink with skating fools. Play spirited music — polkas, kazotzkas, Khachaturian's Saber Dance. Invite a Little League team to join you — just for the fun of it.

Gourmet Gathering

Take over a restaurant for a Sunday afternoon dinner. Invite all your friends. Make sure that they will enjoy one of three different entrees that the restaurant is prepared to offer. Ask them to state their choice of entree when they RSVP. Because you are taking over the whole restaurant you should be able to get the meals at a bargain rate. If that's not possible, contract for a room or a section of the restaurant. Ask everyone to chip in to hire a gypsy violinist or a magician to go from table to table and do tricks.

Visit To A Flea Market

Each member of the family is given $5 or $50 and they set out to see how many treasures they can acquire for that amount. One of the ground rules is that you have to walk the place first, before buying anything, to see all the alternatives that are available. At the agreed upon time and place, everyone meets for a tailgate picnic or adjourns to someone's home to tally up the results of the shopping spree.

Pinecone Creations

Two or three families go out to a wooded area where there are lots of pine trees. Each person is given a cardboard box, and they collect many different sizes and kinds of pinecones. These are brought back to the starting point, and they all drive back to one family's house. With glue and scotch tape, wires and paints, and maybe buttons and beads, they make marvelous things using the pinecones — creating, inventing, designing, helping each other. The group makes Christmas tree ornaments, window decorations, wind chimes, and whatever occurs to anyone. When all is done, the creations are taken to an agency that distributes gifts to poor people. Or they can be taken to a hospital where sick children can enjoy them.

Wood-Gathering Day

A great way to spend a Sunday afternoon is to gather wood.

Complete with chain saw, hand saw and buck saw, and whatever else you may need, go out to a place where trees can be cut. There are some state lands that have cutting privileges. Or perhaps you have a friend who has an old wooded lot and will allow you to cut some of it. The family gathers and rounds up dead trees and kindling wood, dragging branches and trunks to a place where they can be safely cut to size. The car, truck, station wagon or van is filled with as much wood as the family can gather on a Sunday afternoon. Some piles are made to come back and get later on. And everyone looks forward to the warm, wonderful fires ahead that this wood will fuel. And in fact, that's the best way to end the day — making a fire to roast popcorn and marshmallows.

Build A Playground

First you get permission from the owner. Then several families, preferably with teenagers, go to an empty lot which is pretty much an eyesore. They spend some time cleaning out the empty lot and then begin building simple wooden ladder-like structures. Maybe somebody has collected a bunch of old pallets used in warehouses or supermarkets. These can be nailed together in a kind of rough design, and make a wonderful place for climbing and jumping.

Part of the fun of this is total anonymity — the project is done as quickly as possible — and suddenly when people appear the next morning, it's built. It's important to take a picture of it, and to go back sometime to watch children play on what you've built, and laugh about the group of gnomes who put it together. Then you can start looking for another empty lot for another Sunday project.

Neighborhood Bike Hike

This is a special adventure that needs to be experienced at least twice a year. Someone organizes everyone in the neighborhood who has a bicycle for a trip to an amusement park, a beach or an ice cream shop. The destination should not be too far away because there will surely be children in the group. Four or five miles should be the maximum.

Flower Planting

This has a lot of whimsy to it. You go into a state park — or city or county owned land — and plant flower seeds. In the North you can buy seeds and bulbs for tulips and daffodils and plant them in the early fall. The plantings will be in places where people can see them but where they are not normally planted. You cover up the ground very carefully so there is no evidence that you've been there. But you mark the spot well and photograph it. Then when you go back in the spring and photograph it again, it has all turned into a flowery abundance. In warmer spots of the country, you can see the results of your spadework within only a few weeks.

Let's Go Snorkeling

Some Sunday afternoons are bright and sunny — just made for water sports, and for taking family and friends for a snorkeling adventure. It doesn't have to be a Caribbean reef; there are some wonderful places to snorkel along riverbanks, lake shores, any place at all where you might see baby fish swimming in the bottom grass, crayfish or some frogs. It's just a simple matter of putting your head under water to see the miraculous bottom of a pond, lake, riverbank or seashore. If everyone doesn't have a snorkel mask, those who do can share. Later, you can sit around and make a catalogue of everything you've seen in the wonderful world underwater.

Rainy Day Skin Treatment

This is the kind of party that you organize with just a few quick phone calls. It's a rainy day, and the kids say, "What can we do?" You say, "I know what we'll do, we'll call up some other families and have their kids come over, and we'll organize a skin nourishment session." This means simple massages which are usually given by participants to each other. These are described in the book *Caring, Feeling, Touching* by Sidney B. Simon. It tells you how to do exercises and what to say to get everything going just right. It's a wonderful idea and both kids and grown-ups will be so glad that it was a rainy day.

Shooting Birds

Friends with cameras join you at a place where lots of birds live — a nature preserve is just the thing. You walk the woods and trails looking for birds, trying to be as quiet as possible, setting up your tripods and using telephoto lenses to capture your subjects. There is an incredible wildlife refuge on Sanibel Island in Florida, where on a good day you can shoot roseate spoonbills, wood storks and a variety of herons, and where you can see ibis and ducks galore — and every now and then a magnificent alligator. But you, too, will know of a place where birds gather, perhaps in Massachusetts where hawks fly by at certain times of the year, or New York and Connecticut where thousands of ducks and geese come together. Each of you knows of a place where you can see migrating birds — a duck pond or someplace where they return every year. What a wonderful thing it is to photograph as many as you can, and later share your slides and enjoy each other's photographs. This is a wonderful way to introduce children to respect for nature and the beauty of birds.

Deer-Feeding Day

On a winter day in the north, a rewarding way to spend a Sunday afternoon is to feed the wild deer.

This would be when there's been a particular cold snap and you're worried about your deer friends. You load up the station wagon or a pickup truck with bales of hay and some bags of crushed corn, and whatever else you have that deer can eat. This is a wonderful chance to get rid of some very soft and slightly rotten apples because deer love them. You look in the woods for deer tracks, and see where they've been trying to eat the bark off trees. (When deer are desperate, they'll eat anything as far as their necks can reach.) A good place to put the feed is alongside a pond because deer often feed on the trees near ponds by standing on the ice and reaching up. Your deer friends will really welcome your contributions to their winter diet and you will have an afternoon of rosy cheeks, pink noses and deep satisfaction from knowing that you are helping to keep alive an animal population; and making their winter easier.

Tracking Wildlife

Bring along a wild animal expert, or at least a chart that allows you to identify various tracks in the woods. Literally any wooded area near your home will provide tracks for you. You'll see rabbit, raccoon, possibly porcupine and deer, and in some places you may well see a fox, panther or mountain cougar, and maybe even a bear track. It's wonderful to teach kids the joys of tracking animals. Just for fun, you could fashion fake footprints, maybe Bigfoot or the incredible swamp monster, and plant them out in the woods the day before and see how the kids react before you let them in on the joke.

Neighborhood Olympics

The traditional Special Olympics is a series of athletic contests for handicapped children. Here's our own version for all the kids in the neighborhood: You set up a makeshift arena by hanging some rope from a tree limb for climbing races, a swing to see who can swing the highest and so forth. You don't have the usual dashes, swimming or diving events, but you do have obstacle courses, and all the kids get a chance to practice and compete. Competition is by age groups and everybody wins a prize for something. And for one Sunday afternoon everyone has the Olympic spirit.

A Park Happening

Send an invitation to about 500 people, some of whom you know, some of whom are just picked at random. The invitations ask everyone to meet at a certain spot in a park on a Sunday afternoon.

Everyone will be identified by wearing a purple T-shirt on which a phrase is painted, such as *Much Madness Is Divinest Sense To A Discerning Eye — Emily Dickinson*. Let the event proceed from there in whatever direction it happens to go. Everyone brings refreshments — enough to share — and a little common sense. The only rule is that whatever happens should be legal and safe.

PART IV

Fully
Delightful
Complete
Weekends

Complete Weekends

Friday nights, Saturday nights or Sunday afternoons sometimes are just too limiting. There's not enough time in a night or an afternoon to do some really neat things. You may need the entire weekend.

Here are some ideas for whole weekends.

Raft Trip

One of our friends, Matt Weinstein, has an annual raft trip with his friends and the employees of his company, Playfair. They pick a river, find a "river-running" company that's experienced, and go on an extended river-run with food, camping, music and laughter. It's another big commitment, but a lifetime of memories and a wonderful way to keep colleagues close and caring.

Variations: a canoe trip, a backpacking trip, snow-camping or other camping trips with guides.

Book Trip

Do you have lots of books you've purchased but haven't made time to read? We do. Our interest in books always seems to be larger than our reading time. What a relaxing weekend to just go away to a restful place (choose the hotel or inn that advertises no organized activities) and bring along your books. We recommend acquiring one of the excellent guides to bed and breakfast inns for your area. Seek secluded, quiet, scenic places. Look for cozy fireplaces.

Building Projects

In the great American rural tradition, when a neighbor had a big project such as replacing a barn that had burned, the whole community would gather for a barn raising. In one day, the many hands and helpers would put up the whole building. There'd be food, laughter, much play and lots of good work. Why not retrieve this tradition, dust it off, and help a neighbor? Get together and clean up a vacant lot in your neighborhood. Many local hunger centers or shelters appreciate volunteers who come and make sandwiches or bring ones already made. Ask the center how you can help in other ways. If you're a skilled handy person, join the Habitat for

Humanity movement that builds decent housing for people living in disadvantaged neighborhoods.

Volunteering In Groups

A whole weekend can become a very sweet experience if you and your friends volunteer to help at a rehab center, a hospital, a convalescent home or geriatric center. There is no end to the places that need help. Members of Hanoch's synagogue volunteer to staff a hunger center or food bank one night each month. And local churches cooperate to fill many of the other nights. Just look around your town; you'll see the need. Fill it, and it will fill you!

Build A Kit

Buy a kit. Build it. Do it as a group project or as a partner project with the person you love. It doesn't matter what the kit is, just the fact that you're working together will provide all the fun. Just don't let the little "perfectionist demon" that many of us have spoil the fun.

Theme Weekends

Pick a theme and follow it for a whole weekend. For example, if you choose "Cathedrals And Other Beautiful Houses Of Worship" and begin to plan a tour of your area, you will find unexpected beauty and nourishment for your spirit. Visit these places with reverence and, of course, dress appropriately. Synagogues, mosques and Buddhist temples are all possibilities. These visits will teach you a lot about the history, ethnicity and values of the area.

"The Play's The Thing"

Gather a group of friends and spend a weekend preparing a play. Get enough copies of the script. Build scenery. Create costumes. Cast the drama. Choose a director. Practice lines. Get the lighting just right. Put on the play for yet another group of friends the next weekend. Ask the local retirement community or a hospital if they would enjoy seeing your entertainment. Choose a 'mellerdrammer' or a corny comedy from the twenties for extra fun!

Learning A New Skill Weekend

Immersion is one of the best ways to really learn something. Get your trusty group of friends together or propose this idea to a singles group you've joined or another group that may be interested. Chip in and hire a teacher who can give you intensive instruction on something you've always wanted to learn. You might take a crash course in karate, Spanish, ballroom dancing, country swing, ice-skating, knitting, quilting, antique buying or investment strategies. There's no limit.

How Far Can You Go?

This is a contest that a group of couples can play. There's an agreed-upon budget. You may not spend more on actual travel costs (gas, food, lodging, airfare, etc.) than the budgeted amount. Each couple leaves Friday night or Saturday morning. You must return by 6 o'clock Sunday night and meet at one central location and compare notes. Which couple went the farthest on the least amount of money?

Visit-Hopping

It's a variation on the "progressive dinner" party. You have drinks in one couple's home, appetizers in the next, main dish in a third and desert in a fourth home. You can do lots of variations of this idea. Breakfast in home #1, biking near home #2; lunch in home #3; swimming at home #4, dinner at home #5 and so forth.

Rummage Rampage

Some of the best shoppers know the out-of-the-way places, such as "Ye Olde Junque Shoppe" that has the neatest things but looks so scuzzy that you might never have stopped to check. Everyone divulges their favorite weird bargain source. Go together from one to the next.

Auction Action

Many great days and evenings can be spent at farm auctions and sales. In more rural areas, these are really the interesting community events. You'll be interacting with new people and you'll learn a great deal about the community, its history and values. You'll pick up some fabulous bargains, too!

Theater Overload Weekend

This is one of our favorites. Sid and Suzanne Simon "invented" it and we've learned from them. They spend a lot of time planning this one. They check *The New York Times* on Sunday for months, reading the play reviews. Bit by bit, they plan out how to spend their weekend. This play on Thursday night, that one on Friday night, then there's the Saturday matinee at an off-Broadway play. Saturday night is a play, too. And so is Sunday afternoon! Exhausted, filled with ideas and drama and poetry, they return to their home in Massachusetts. Of course, they've bought tickets through a broker and via phone from the ticket agencies and theaters. They've learned that there's a "twofer" service which sells tickets "on the cheap" if you're willing to stand in line in Times Square. We do this same idea in San Francisco. Can you get to a large city near you? It's a memorable way to spend a weekend. And you can sneak in some quick shopping at the special stores of your choice, too.

Cross-Country Inn Tour

There are, in New England, a number of inns that advertise tours in Sunday's *New York Times Magazine* as well as other places. The idea is to go to a country inn, have dinner and stay the night. In the morning, pack up. Your car remains at this inn. Your luggage is loaded in a van to be brought to the next inn. A guide takes you and a group on a cross-country skiing trek, over hills and dales, to the next inn, which may be twenty miles away. There are appropriate rest stops and lunches. When you get to the next inn, you have dinner and find your luggage already in a nice warm room! And so it goes for several days. Are you in shape for this? It's a magical way to see New England, but it's not for beginning skiers.

One Last Thought

Until now you were probably a member of the "Two-Rut Society." There was the Monday through Friday rut: inching along on a crowded expressway or running to catch a train or bus; the job routine, the evening crawl along the "Interstate parking lot" or the getting up close and personal with a gazillion other folks in a sardine can on wheels; dinner, TV and bed.

On Saturday you stepped into the weekend rut: the obligatory trip to the mall in the morning and the squeezing into a crowded restaurant or night club at night. Sunday you parked yourself in front of the TV and became a couch potato.

Admittedly, there isn't much anyone can do about the weekday routine. But now, after having read (or even tried) some of our "rut-busters," you can see that there really is life after Friday. Enjoy.

Calling
All Recreators!

We've got a good head start on planning fun, interesting weekends. With your help, we'd like to keep the party going! Send us a letter or postcard and share your special weekend activity: a fun Friday, a superb Saturday, a spirited Sunday or your best weekend package. Describe your agenda as clearly as you can and, with your permission, we'll use it in our next newsletter or book on weekends.

Send your ideas to us at the following address:

Hanoch McCarty and Sidney B. Simon
P.O. Box 66
Galt, California 95632

We'll credit you for your contribution, so be certain to print your name, address and phone number on your letter so that we may do so correctly. Together, we can unshackle ourselves from the drudgery of weekend chores. Let leisure reign!

About
The Authors

Hanoch McCarty has been speaking professionally for over 27 years all over the world. He is the President of Hanoch McCarty & Associates, a seminar and training company that helps companies, schools, organizations and individuals reach their goals and achieve their fullest potential congruent with their highest integrity.

Hanoch conducts on-site training for corporations, government agencies, school districts and professional associations. He also presents public seminars and sponsored workshops for parent groups, individuals and institutions all across America. He has delivered keynote addresses at hundreds of national, regional, statewide and local conventions and meetings. He has received many, many standing ovations for his phenomenal, exciting and unique style and thought-provoking messages.

Hanoch creates *custom-designed* presentations ensuring that there will be material relevant to the audience, its concerns, needs and special experiences. He has a wide variety of tape programs, video trainings and books available. If you would like to receive a brochure and a free demo tape describing his work, please call 1-800-231-7353 or write P.O. Box 66, Galt, CA 95632.

Sidney Simon has been a pioneer in psychological education. While his workshops have been critically acclaimed for years, he continues to develop new and exciting ones for his audiences. Most recently they have been delivered with his wife, *Changes* columnist Suzanne Simon, on the topic of forgiveness and breaking cycles. Sid also has the unique honor and distinction of doing workshops with two of his grown children. He does Fathers and Daughters workshops with his daughter Julianna Simon, and Fathers and Sons workshops with his son John Simon. To get on their mailing lists contact Sidney at: 1757 Venus Drive, Sanibel, FL 33957.

Books To Set Your Spirit Free

Chicken Soup For The Soul
101 Stories To Open The Heart
And Rekindle The Spirit
Jack Canfield and Mark Victor Hansen

Here is a treasury of 101 stories collected by two of America's best-loved inspirational speakers. Metaphors for life's deep and profound truths, these stories provide models for what is possible, give us permission to be more fully human, and illuminate and clarify the path we walk. Just what the doctor ordered to heal your soul and put a smile on your face.

Code 262X (paperback) **$12.00**
Code 2913 (cloth) **$20.00**

Acts Of Kindness
How To Create
A Kindness Revolution
Meladee McCarty and Hanoch McCarty

The long-overdue kindness revolution is sweeping the country and is waiting for you to enlist! This delightful book tells you everything you need to know to perform intentional acts of kindness for your family, friends, co-workers, schoolmates, strangers and people in need. With ideas and directions for over 100 heart-warming things to do, you'll never run out of ways to spread sunshine.

Code 2956 . . . . **$10.00**

3201 S.W. 15th Street
Deerfield Beach, FL 33442-9879
1-800-441-5569

Health
Communications, Inc.®